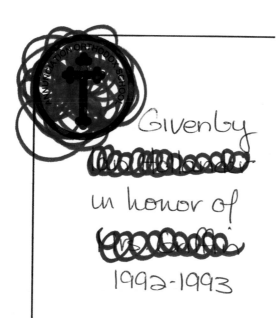

THE ROSENBERGS

by

Anita Larsen

Illustrated by
Marcy Ramsey

CRESTWOOD HOUSE
NEW YORK

Maxwell Macmillan Canada
Toronto

Maxwell Macmillan International
New York   Oxford   Singapore   Sydney

Library of Congress Cataloging-in-Publication Data
Larsen, Anita.

The Rosenbergs / by Anita Larsen. — 1st ed.
p. cm. — (History's mysteries)
Includes bibliographical references and index.
Summary: In one of the twentieth century's most controversial trials, the Rosenbergs defend themselves against the U.S. government's charges that they passed atomic bomb secrets to the Soviet Union.
ISBN 0-89686-612-2
1. Rosenberg, Julius, 1918–1953—Trials, litigation, etc.—Juvenile literature. 2. Rosenberg, Ethel, 1915–1953—Trials, litigation, etc.—Juvenile literature. 3. Trials (Espionage)—New York (N.Y.)—Juvenile literature. 4. Trials (Conspiracy)—New York (N.Y.)—Juvenile literature. [1. Rosenberg, Julius, 1918–1953. 2. Rosenberg, Ethel, 1915–1953. 3. Communists. 4. Trials (Espionage). 5. Trials (Conspiracy).] I. Title. II. Series.
KF224.R6L37 1992
345.73'0231—dc20
[347.305231]   91-22311
                                                                                                                          CIP
                                                                                                                          AC

Crestwood House
Macmillan Publishing Company
866 Third Avenue
New York, NY 10022

Maxwell Macmillan Canada, Inc.
1200 Eglinton Avenue East
Suite 200
Don Mills, Ontario M3C 3N1

Macmillan Publishing Company is part of the Maxwell Communication Group of Companies.

First edition

Printed in the United States of America

10 9 8 7 6 5 4 3 2 1

CONTENTS

▲▲▲▲▲▲▲▲▲▲▲▲▲▲▲▲▲▲▲▲▲▲▲▲▲▲▲▲▲▲▲▲▲▲▲

THE CASE OPENS

▲▲▲▲▲▲▲▲▲▲▲▲▲▲▲▲▲▲▲▲▲▲▲▲▲▲▲▲▲▲▲

It is Friday, June 19, 1953.

Convicted spies Julius and Ethel Rosenberg will be electrocuted today in New York State's Sing Sing Prison unless something happens to stop it.

The day is hot, humid and tense. Sixty New York State troopers have joined prison guards and local police to patrol the prison walls. Emotions in the Rosenberg case are running high, and a demonstration is possible. Roads leading to the prison are barricaded.

Thirty reporters wait in the prison's stifling visitors' room for news from the death house. The FBI has set up a secret command post with a direct line to headquarters in the warden's garage. The FBI hopes that one or both of the Rosenbergs will break and confess to selling atomic secrets to the Russians.

The Rosenbergs have already said good-bye to family members. On Tuesday, June 16, they saw their sons in the prison counsel room. There they hugged and kissed ten-year-old Michael and six-year-old Robert. Ethel read aloud a letter begging mercy from President Dwight D. Eisenhower. He still might grant executive clemency and keep them from dying in the electric chair.

The Rosenbergs tried to play calmly with their sons and make this visit an ordinary one. But the strain was too great. Michael began acting up. Shattered, Ethel kissed her sons, promised to write them a last letter, and ran from the room.

The next day, June 17, Julius's mother, brother and sister came. They were there at 11:30 A.M. when the prison loudspeaker squawked. It was hopeful news.

Supreme Court Justice William O. Douglas had independently ordered a stay, or delay, of execution. He saw legal grounds to do so. The Rosenbergs had been sentenced under the Espionage Act of 1917. The Atomic Energy Act of 1946 cancelled out the earlier law. Under the 1946 law, a death sentence could be imposed only if the jury recommended it. The jury had listened to the evidence and didn't impose it.

But a 6:00 P.M. loudspeaker announcement dashed the Rosenbergs' hopes. The attorney general of the United States had asked the Supreme Court to meet the next day to reaffirm its earlier ruling. If the court did so, then it would block Douglas's order. The Rosenbergs would die.

The next day was Thursday, June 18, the Rosenbergs' 14th wedding anniversary. They celebrated by preparing for the worst. They saw the prison's Jewish chaplain, Rabbi Irving Koslowe. They waited nervously for word from the court.

The next morning, Friday, they hear the court has voted six to three to execute.

Less than an hour later, President Eisenhower refuses executive clemency for the second time. The attorney general orders the Rosenbergs' execution at 8:00 P.M. The usual execution time is 11:00 P.M. but the time is put forward so the couple won't die on the Jewish Sabbath, which begins at sundown.

With less than a day to live, Ethel writes to thank their attorney. She writes to her sons. Always remember we are innocent, she says. She leaves them all she has—two pieces of jewelry.

Julius spends the afternoon and early evening outside Ethel's cell, as usual. At 7:20 P.M. he is taken

into another room. His head is partially shaved so the electrodes can be applied. So is one leg. His pants leg is slit to accommodate the wire.

The rabbi appears. Julius follows him, escorted by two guards. The rabbi chants the 23rd Psalm: "The Lord is my shepherd, I shall not want."

At 8:00 P.M. Julius Rosenberg enters the white glare of the death chamber. He sits in the oak chair. The electrodes are applied. His arms and legs are strapped down. After the standard three jolts of electricity, he is pronounced dead. It is 8:06 P.M.

While the death chamber is cleared, the rabbi comes to Ethel. Confess, he begs, for your children's sake. She refuses.

The two matrons Ethel has requested as her escort come to her cell. She follows the rabbi, who now chants the 31st Psalm: "In thee, O Lord, do I put my trust; let me never be ashamed. . . . For I have heard the slander of many. . . . They devised to take away my life."

She enters the death chamber and turns impulsively to her escorts. One reaches for Ethel's outstretched hand and draws near. Ethel kisses her on the check, and the matron is overcome. She dashes from the room. Ethel shakes the other matron's hand and watches her leave.

As the electrodes and straps are applied, Ethel stares at the impassive faces before her. The United States marshal, his chief deputy, the warden, the executioner, two doctors and three wire-service reporters chosen to represent the media stare back. A witness later said she had "the most composed look you ever saw."

At 8:11 P.M. three currents surge through Ethel's body. A white plume of smoke rises from her head. But she does not die. Two more shocks are needed before she can be pronounced dead. It is 8:16 P.M.

The Rosenbergs' attorney makes a statement: "This was an act of cold, deliberate murder. . . . This was not American justice. . . . This was the face of Nazism."

Throughout Europe people mourn the Rosenbergs' deaths as fervently as they had earlier rallied to prevent them.

Many Americans feel relief. The "soldiers of Stalin," as Ethel's mother put it, are no longer a threat. They agree with Judge Irving Kaufman, who said as he sentenced Ethel that she had committed a "crime worse than murder." They agree that her actions were instrumental in starting the Korean War.

Others think differently. A *National Guardian* editorial calls the Rosenbergs' execution a crime "which stains America's name before the world."

The Rosenberg controversy has never died. Were they guilty? Or were they innocent?

THE CASE FILE
▲▲▲▲▲▲▲▲▲▲▲▲▲▲▲▲▲▲▲▲▲▲▲▲▲▲▲▲▲▲

UNEXCEPTIONAL LIVES

The Rosenbergs' attorney said that the couple had led unexceptional lives. Both had grown up in squalid tenements in New York City's Lower East Side, but they didn't meet until they were adults.

Julius, the youngest of his family, was born on May 12, 1918. The family was poor. When Julius was ten the family moved up to a housing project. For the first time they had heat, lights and a private bathroom.

Julius's father belonged to the garment workers' union. The Rosenbergs taught their children to feel sympathy for the needy. They taught them to believe in equality and justice and to realize that the only escape from poverty was to fight alongside other workers for better pay and working conditions.

Julius was a sickly child. He was encouraged to spend his convalescence doing what he most wanted to do anyway—read. When he was enrolled in Hebrew school, Julius put aside his regular schoolwork to study the Torah for four hours or more every day. He spent Friday evenings and all of Saturday at Hebrew school too. Sometimes his teachers would tell him he was overdoing it.

Religious study continued to be the center of Julius's life until he was a senior in high school. One day he stopped on the street to listen to a speaker from the American Communist Party. The speech was about Tom Mooney, a West Coast labor leader. Many believed Mooney had been jailed on perjured testimony. They said the witnesses had lied under oath. Julius donated his savings—50 cents—to the campaign to free Tom Mooney.

He began going to the communist social center a few blocks from home. There he heard talk about equality and fighting injustice, the same issues of his religious studies. He attempted to gain support from the rabbis for Tom Mooney. When he failed, Julius began to move from religion to politics.

After high school he enrolled in City College of New York to study engineering. The college, then tuition-free, was a center of political activity. Julius joined socialist and communist youth groups. He took a part-time job in a drugstore in a mostly black neighborhood. Even after a childhood of poverty, he was shocked at the overcrowding, high rents and high prices in the local white-owned stores.

One night a bus ran over a black man. The bleeding man was brought into the drugstore. In the hour it took for the ambulance to arrive, the man died. Julius mopped up the blood and swore never to forget this "crime." At the time only the Communist Party spoke out against racism. By late December 1936 Julius was one of thousands who were wrapped up in the communist movement.

Ethel Greenglass was born on September 28, 1915. She joined her half brother, Sammy, in the family's cold-water flat. One of the differences between the early lives of Ethel and Julius was that Ethel was a girl—and therefore immediately less valuable in this ghetto society than a boy. Rather than being the favored "baby" of the family, Ethel was a thorn in its side.

The only good Tessie Greenglass could see in her daughter was that, at six and a half years of age, Ettie was a good "second mother" to her youngest brother, David, called Doovey, and even at times to her next youngest brother, Bernie.

"Little motherhood" was the only education girls needed, Tessie thought. Formal education was for boys. Shy, quiet Ettie pored over her schoolbooks anyway. The pleasure of earning good grades and compliments from teachers eased the pain of life at home.

But success in school only made more trouble at home. Her brothers weren't as bright as Ethel. Her mother had no accomplishments. Everybody's shortcomings became Ethel's faults. The only pleasant family times were when Ethel and her father, Barney, a sewing-machine repairman, went to the Yiddish theaters dotting the area.

By the time she was in high school, Ethel dreamed of being an actress and singer, or going to college.

But the 1930s were not good times for a poor girl to pay for a college education. After she graduated from high school in 1931, Ethel took a clerical day job. She acted in amateur productions at night. She sang in an amateur-night competition and won the $2 second-place prize—good money in the Great Depression.

Ethel wanted singing lessons. Tessie said no. With typical determination, Ethel found someone who would give their piano to anyone who would

cart it away. She brought the small upright piano home and taught herself to play it while she sang. Her mother screamed at her to stop the noise.

Ethel decided to audition for the Schola Cantorum, a citywide chorus that performed in Carnegie Hall. She had to learn to sight-read music for that. She taught herself, and in 1935 19-year-old Ethel was accepted—as the chorus's youngest member.

The same year she joined a labor union. She was being paid less than other women who were doing the same work. When the union went on strike in August 1935, Ethel supported the action.

One night, as Ethel and a group of fellow strikers walked home from a meeting, a group of men hired by the company sprang at them. They beat the strikers to the sidewalk with iron pipes, then vanished. For the first time Ethel thought the communists were right: There was a class struggle.

The strike was settled, and everyone returned to work. But Ethel and other members of the strike committee were soon fired. They appealed their case to the new National Labor Relations Board. Months later, they won. By this time, however, Ethel had found another job.

She also went on singing with the Schola Cantorum and was often asked to sing at local

political events. One of these was a holiday benefit for the International Seamen's Union in December 1936.

LOVE STORY

The night of the Seamen's benefit, a handsome man with gray-green eyes and an endearing smile was in the audience. He'd told 21-year-old Ethel that he was a college sophomore earlier. She was impressed.

Eighteen-year-old Julius Rosenberg, the guy with gray-green eyes, listened to Ethel sing. He was impressed.

Julius helped Ethel from the stage when she had finished, telling her she had the most beautiful voice he'd ever heard. The two left together that night. They began turning up at the same political meetings, leaving arm in arm. They were married on June 18, 1939.

Ethel was offered a job in the Census Bureau in Washington, D.C., even though a mysterious phone call to her employers had advised them of her politics. The couple moved to Washington in June 1940, and Julius began looking for work. An appointment as a junior engineer for the army signal corps came through. He would start training in New Jersey right after Labor Day that year. Ethel would join him in New York on October 1, after she had given notice at her job.

Julius's job required travel, which took him away from Ethel too often. But he liked the chance to convert people in the workplace to communism. His politics required that.

He recruited openly, then was surprised to be called for a loyalty hearing in January 1941. Called again on March 8, Julius lied under oath about his Communist Party affiliation. He convinced the hearing officer that he wasn't a communist and was able to return to work. He went on recruiting, though less openly now.

World War II had begun in 1939, and the United States was involved in December 1941. The Soviet Union and America were now allies. Ethel took a full-time job with a civilian defense agency. Julius was also busy at work, and the family was economically secure. Their first son, Michael, was born on March 10, 1943. He was a difficult child, and Ethel began suffering from stress-related pain.

In early 1945 Julius was in trouble again. The FBI had found concrete evidence of his Communist Party ties, and the army ordered a loyalty investigation. On February 9, 1945, Julius was

placed on "indefinite suspension" from his signal corps job. He found another job, however, researching new military designs for the army and navy.

On August 6, 1945, America dropped the first atomic bomb on the city of Hiroshima, in Japan. Another bomb was dropped on Nagasaki three days later. The bombs ended the war.

Soldiers came home and married. Suburbs sprang up across the country. People started to buy cars, homes, appliances. America was riding a tide of rosy prospects, but with the war over, military spending had fallen off. Julius was laid off. His communist background dogged his job search at a time when Ethel was expecting their second child.

Julius had to find work and couldn't. He did the only thing he could: start his own business. His brothers-in-law Bernie and David Greenglass joined him.

The company struggled from the beginning. Family hostilities arose. Because of his politics, there was little hope that Julius could find a different job. By the time their second son, Robert, was born on May 14, 1947, Ethel was buying food on credit at the grocery store.

COLD WAR/HOT HEADS

Bad feelings about communism and America's former ally, the Soviet Union, began in the United States almost as soon as Nazi Germany was defeated in 1945. Russia's brutality toward its World War II enemies and its own people at home frightened Americans. What if the brutal Russians bombed America?

Just before the 1946 elections, the U.S. Chamber of Commerce published a 38-page pamphlet titled *Communist Infiltration in the United States: Its Nature and How to Combat It.* The pamphlet was intended to show that the New Deal programs of Democratic president Franklin Roosevelt had laid the groundwork for a communist takeover in the United States. In January 1947 the pamphlet was expanded into a 57-page booklet.

The Communist Party had been a legal political party in the United States before World War II. By the 1950s, however, citizens could be prosecuted for membership. The word *communist* became synonymous with *Russian spy.* The House Un-American Activities Committee (HUAC), led by Senator Joseph McCarthy, held hearings to ferret out communists. "Are you now, or have you ever been, a member of the Communist Party?" he asked.

People who answered yes were blacklisted. They couldn't find jobs.

Some of the people who came before McCarthy's committee "took the Fifth." The Fifth Amendment to the United States Constitution says that people do not have to testify or give evidence against themselves. It allows people to refuse to answer a question on the grounds that their answer might tend to incriminate them. But taking the Fifth at that time was also often seen as an admission that a person had something to hide.

In many cases people who took the Fifth thought that McCarthy's hearings were meaningless since so many Americans had been communists during the Depression. Communism at that time was an economic philosophy. It called for ownership and distribution of property, products and income by a community rather than by individuals. It was not a political program for the overthrow of the government.

Other witnesses were happy to "name names" for McCarthy. Elizabeth Bentley, a self-confessed courier for the Communist Party, named over 80 names—so many that the media called her the "Red Spy Killer." She later testified against the Rosenbergs.

The "red scare" hysteria grew. The Internal Security Act of 1950 made political beliefs—not just actions—illegal. It also allowed for the creation of concentration camps for subversives during "national emergencies." Senator John McClellan even called for an atomic strike against Russia so that America could "become the first aggressor for peace." In schools across the nation, students practiced bomb drills as well as fire drills.

ACCUSED!

On Monday, July 17, 1950, the Rosenbergs faced something more frightening than shaky finances.

As the boys listened to "The Lone Ranger," a man came into the room and switched off the radio. More men came to search the apartment. The boys heard their mother screaming. "I want a lawyer!" she insisted. Then she took them into the bedroom. Michael asked if their father would be home that night. "No, not tonight," Ethel said. Julius had been arrested.

Soon neighbors wouldn't enter the same elevator with Ethel. Almost totally alone, Ethel was also thrust into managing a failing business. She had seldom written even a personal check before.

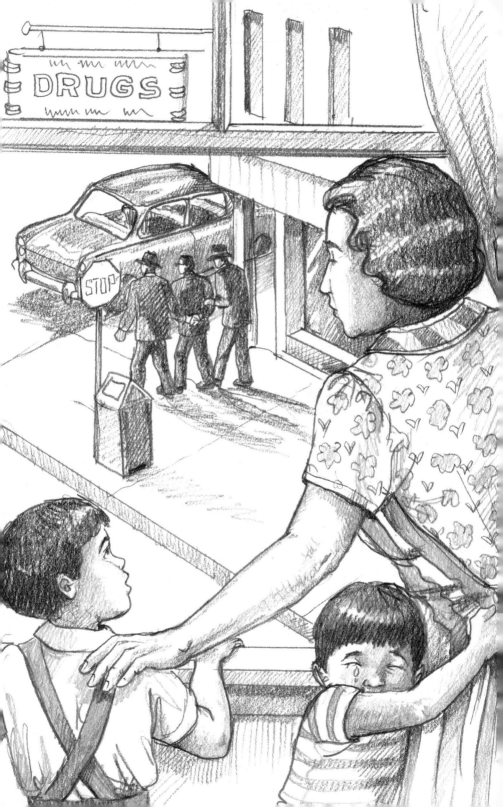

On August 7 she was called before a grand jury. Irving Saypol, the prosecuting attorney, had decided that pressuring Ethel might push Julius into confessing. Julius's attorney, Emanuel Bloch, advised Ethel to take the Fifth.

After her first hearing Ethel was told to return on August 11. Worried about her children, she went home and called the Jewish Community Homemakers Service to find a foster family. She made an appointment for the day of her grand jury appearance.

On August 11 Ethel left the grand jury, heading for the meeting about her children. Two FBI agents stopped her. "You'll have to come with us," they said. "You're under arrest." Like Julius, she had been charged with conspiracy to commit espionage.

THE TRIAL

The FBI investigation of the Rosenbergs began when agents found the name Klaus Fuchs scribbled in a Russian spy's notebook. German-born Dr. Fuchs was a naturalized British citizen. From 1943 to 1946 he had worked with British and American scientists on the top-secret Manhattan Project. This mission at Los Alamos, New Mexico, had resulted in the atomic bomb. When Dr. Fuchs was arrested, he confessed that he had been passing information to the Russians.

The thread ran from Dr. Fuchs to Harry Gold, a Philadelphia biochemist. Gold said his Soviet contact, Anatoli A. Yakovlev, had told him to meet Fuchs in Santa Fe, New Mexico, on June 2, 1945. Fuchs would turn over scientific information that included data about the implosion lens. This device detonated the bomb. Gold said he was told to go from Santa Fe to Albuquerque. There he'd get drawings of the lens from an ex-army sergeant, now a machinist at Los Alamos. Yakovlev allegedly gave Gold the password—"I come from Julius"— along with the contact's name and address and a section torn from a Jell-O box. Matching sections would be identification.

At first Gold told the FBI he couldn't remember the contact's name, but he gave them a description. The FBI showed him a number of photos. One was of David Greenglass, who was in the FBI files because he'd been investigated in January 1950 for having stolen some uranium from Los Alamos as a souvenir. He had been working there as a machinist. Greenglass's photo "resembled" the man he'd met, Gold said. A week later, Gold said that David was the man.

Gold's story was this: The Greenglasses weren't home when he arrived at their Albuquerque house. He checked into a tourist home for the night. The next morning, June 3, he checked into the Hilton Hotel, then returned to the Greenglasses' house. The Jell-O box pieces were matched, the password given, and David's sketches handed over. Gold boarded a train that evening and reached New York on June 5. He gave the material from Fuchs and Greenglass to Yakovlev at their prearranged 10:00 P.M. meeting.

The FBI sent films of Gold to Fuchs, who was in prison in England. Fuchs identified Gold. So did "Red Spy Killer" Elizabeth Bentley. Gold was tried, found guilty and given a 30-year sentence.

The FBI called in David Greenglass for questioning. A teenaged David had idolized his brother-in-law Julius and had become a communist because of his influence. Now he said Julius was the leader of the spy ring.

The FBI interviewed Max Elitcher, an engineer in the navy. Elitcher had been one of Julius's college classmates. Elitcher's best friend was scientist Morton Sobell. Elitcher said Julius had told him that Sobell was among the scientists giving atomic information to the Soviet Union. This was an inducement to Elitcher to join the spy ring. In August 1950 the FBI moved in on Morton Sobell.

The prosecution's major witnesses were now set. They included David's wife, Ruth. David Greenglass, Morton Sobell and the Rosenbergs were the defendants. The case went to trial on March 5, 1951. The trial lasted 31 days.

Before testimony began, Judge Irving Kaufman told the jury that communism was not on trial. However, one juror later said, "The defense and the judge said that communism was not on trial, but I started to get the impression that communism was on trial." The foreman of the jury said, "In my time a communist was a monster, someone who was going to destroy me and my way of life."

On March 29, 1951, the jury returned verdicts against the defendants: Guilty.

On April 5, 1951, Judge Kaufman passed sentence, telling Ethel her actions had been instrumental in starting the Korean War. She and Julius were given the death sentence.

THE APPEALS

The Rosenbergs' attorney immediately began working on a brief for the circuit court of appeals. The brief contained 25 separate legal points that

could reverse the death sentence.

The appeal was argued on January 10, 1952. A month and a half later, the court filed its opinion. It was bad news for the Rosenbergs.

Because the Greenglasses were both confessed spies, their testimony was suspect, the court said. If the Greenglasses' testimony were ignored, the Rosenbergs' conviction "could not stand." But since the jury had believed the Greenglasses, the court must too.

The appeal had also complained about Judge Kaufman's unfairness. But when defense attorney Bloch summed up his case for the jury, he'd said the trial had been conducted with dignity and decorum. The appeals court could do nothing but reject the complaint.

So it went, with point after legal point. The court noted that the death sentence seemed too harsh. The court was obviously sympathetic to the Rosenbergs, but it was legally helpless to change the sentence. Judge Jerome Frank, a brilliant judge, wrote the opinion. Only the Supreme Court could reduce the harsh sentences, he wrote. But he outlined the legal steps the Rosenbergs could take to avoid death.

In *The Implosion Conspiracy,* attorney Louis Nizer totaled all these appeals. In addition to two denied requests for executive clemency, 112 judges had reviewed the appeals and agreed with the original judgment. Because judges were appointed to various federal courts, the same judges sometimes considered the case more than once. Judges agreed on 112 occasions, rather than 112 different judges agreeing.

Only 16 judges disagreed. Again, this means that judges disagreed on 16 occasions, not that 16 different judges disagreed. None of the dissenting opinions contended that the Rosenbergs were innocent. The disagreements were legalistic, dealing with whether a stay or a further review should be granted.

LATER DEVELOPMENTS

On November 10, 1952, Julius wrote a letter to his attorney. He said that in exchange for lighter sentences, the prosecution's witnesses told a story in court that the FBI had coached them on. He pointed to strange differences in the sentences:

David Greenglass, a confessed spy, was sentenced to 15 years. Julius Rosenberg received death.

Ruth Greenglass, another confessed spy, was never indicted and was permitted to go free. Ethel Rosenberg was sentenced to death.

Julius's friend Max Elitcher, who was threatened with prosecution for espionage and faced a possible five-year prison term, was never indicted.

Morton Sobell was sentenced to 30 years.

Later discoveries support the idea that the Rosenbergs were innocent. In their 1965 book *Invitation to an Inquest,* Miriam and Walter Schneir studied tapes of Gold's statements to his lawyer. The tapes didn't match Gold's courtroom testimony. Gold never mentioned the Jell-O box to his attorney, and the password was "something like 'Bob sent me' or 'Benny sent me,' rather than 'I come from Julius.' "

The Schneirs also argue that Gold's Hilton Hotel registration card was forged. Dated June 3 on its face, the card was time-stamped June 4 on the back. Hotel officials said the time stamp would be the accurate record. And June 4 was the day Gold claimed he was returning to New York.

Still more confusion arises from David and Ruth Greenglass's almost gleeful testimony against family members. Had they wanted lesser sentences? Or had they wanted to "get" Julius and Ethel because of anger over the family business? In fact, David Greenglass's ability—or lack of it—was a major reason the business was failing. Customers reject bad work. David's work was bad.

Had David's sketches damaged American security? David's Los Alamos boss said at the trial that his sketch of the lens was "substantially an accurate representation." But in 1966 two other atomic scientists involved in the Manhattan Project gave sworn affidavits that the sketch was childish and worthless.

Before and after the trial, key scientists said that even an excellent sketch wouldn't have told the Russians anything they didn't already know. National security was not at risk because there were no atomic "secrets."

The United States government seemed to agree with that idea in 1945, five years before the Rosenbergs were even arrested. That year the *Official Report of the United States Government on Atomic Energy Development for Military Purposes* was published. It was generally agreed that trained scientists could get a clear idea of the bomb's structure from the report. The report was printed as a book, *Atomic Energy for Military Purposes*. A first edition of 30,000 copies was printed in the Soviet Union.

People who believe in the Rosenbergs' innocence say that national security wasn't the issue in their trial. These people point to power struggles between the Republican and Democratic parties. They say that the media rushed to present stories that boosted sales because they frightened Americans. The stories were so convincing that a majority of Americans favored death for "traitors."

You have just read the known facts about one of HISTORY'S MYSTERIES. To date, there have been no more answers to the mysteries posed in the story. There are possibilities, though. Read on and see which answer seems the most believable to you. How would you solve the case?

SOLUTIONS

▲▲▲▲▲▲▲▲▲▲▲▲▲▲▲▲▲▲▲▲▲▲▲▲▲▲▲▲▲

GUILTY

The Rosenbergs were guilty of something. Their defense attorneys could have attempted to discredit the prosecution's contradictory testimony on cross-examination. They could have called in witnesses to refute testimony. They did not.

Julius Rosenberg's testimony can't be relied upon. He'd lied under oath before. During his second loyalty hearing he committed perjury in order to keep his job in the army signal corps.

The number of judicial reviews during the Rosenberg appeals alone means the two were guilty. Incredible legal care was taken in the case. The court bent over backward to give the Rosenbergs every chance—and still found them guilty.

INNOCENT

The Rosenbergs were guilty only of exercising their constitutional rights and responsibilities when they joined the Communist Party in the 1930s. They joined for the same reasons thousands of other Americans did. They continued to be communists in the early 1940s while Russia was an ally of the United States.

When World War II ended in 1945, the Cold War between the Western and Eastern powers began. The Rosenbergs were no better or worse than others. They hid their past political activities so they could work and raise their families.

The Republican party wanted to return to the White House after long years of a Democratic presidency. That led to the "red spy scare" in the late 1940s and early 1950s. The media whipped up public sentiment, which allowed the excesses of the House Un-American Activities Committee, led by Senator Joseph McCarthy.

Research in the 1960s and 1970s shows that the FBI's case against the Rosenbergs contained forged and perjured evidence. There was no way the Korean War could have been caused by Ethel Rosenberg.

CLOSING THE CASE FILE
▲▲▲▲▲▲▲▲▲▲▲▲▲▲▲▲▲▲▲▲▲▲▲▲▲▲▲▲▲

The Rosenbergs were the first convicted spies to be put to death during peacetime. There is a three-year statute of limitations that prevents prosecution if a spy is caught three years after he or she commits espionage. A spy can be tried after three years only if the crime is punishable by death. In 1953, the so-called Rosenberg Law removed the statute of limitations in cases affecting national security. The law made the death penalty possible for peacetime espionage as well as for that committed during wartime.

After the Rosenberg executions in 1953, a National Committee to Reopen the Rosenberg Case was formed. In 1974, 21 years later, enough interest in the case remained for 3,000 people to jam New York City's Carnegie Hall to hear discussions about reopening the case.

Were the Rosenbergs guilty? Or were they innocent? Perhaps their case proves only that Americans can be proud that they have the freedom to ask.

CHRONOLOGY

▲▲▲▲▲▲▲▲▲▲▲▲▲▲▲▲▲▲▲▲▲▲▲▲▲▲▲▲▲▲▲▲▲▲▲▲▲

1915	September 28, Ethel Greenglass is born.
1918	May 12, Julius Rosenberg is born.
1939	June 18, Ethel and Julius marry.
1943	March 10, Michael Rosenberg is born.
1945	May 7, Germany surrenders; Cold War begins.
	August 6, Atomic bomb dropped on Hiroshima, Japan.
	August 9, Atomic bomb dropped on Nagasaki, Japan.
	August 15, Japan surrenders.
	September 8, First U.S. forces enter Korea to replace Japanese forces there.
1947	May 14, Robert Rosenberg is born.
1950	July 17, Julius Rosenberg arrested.
	August 11, Ethel Rosenberg arrested.
1951	March 5, "Rosenberg Spy Ring" trial begins.
	April 5, Sentences handed down.
1953	June 19, Rosenbergs are executed.
1974	National Committee to Reopen the Rosenberg Case is formed.

RESOURCES

▲▲▲▲▲▲▲▲▲▲▲▲▲▲▲▲▲▲▲▲▲▲▲▲▲▲▲▲▲▲▲▲

SOURCES

Meeropol, Robert, and Michael Meeropol. *We Are Your Sons.* Boston: Houghton Mifflin Company, 1975.

Nizer, Louis. *The Implosion Conspiracy.* New York: Doubleday, 1973.

Philipson, Ilene. *Ethel Rosenberg: Beyond the Myths.* New York: Franklin Watts, 1988.

Schneir, Walter, and Miriam Schneir. *Invitation to an Inquest.* New York: Doubleday, 1965.

FURTHER READING FOR YOUNG READERS

Silverstein, Herman. *Spies Among Us: The Truth About Modern Espionage.* New York: Franklin Watts, 1988.

INDEX

▲▲▲▲▲▲▲▲▲▲▲▲▲▲▲▲▲▲▲▲▲▲▲▲▲▲▲▲▲▲▲▲▲▲▲▲▲▲